Published by
ORO Editions
Publishers of Architecture, Art, and Design
Gordon Goff: Publisher
www.oroeditions.com
info@oroeditions.com

Edited by: Sorg Architects
Book design by Circular Studio:
Pablo Mandel, art direction; Horacio Pozzo, design
This book has been typesetted in Benton Sans: a neo-grotesque typeface, differing from other realist, more severe sans-serifs in that its organic shapes and subtler transitions of stroke width contribute to the milder impression of a humanist tone of voice.

Color Separations and Printing: ORO Group Ltd.
Printed in China.

This book was printed and bound using a variety of sustainable manufacturing processes and materials including soy-based inks, acqueous-based varnish, VOC- and formaldehyde-free glues, and phthalate-free laminations. The text is printed using offset sheetfed lithographic printing process in (book specific) color on 157gsm premium matte art paper with an off-line gloss acqueous spot varnish applied to all photographs.

ORO Editions makes a continuous effort to minimize the overall carbon footprint of its publications. As part of this goal, ORO Editions, in association with Global ReLeaf, arranges to plant trees to replace those used in the manufacturing of the paper produced for its books. Global ReLeaf is an international campaign run by American Forests, one of the world's oldest nonprofit conservation organizations. Global ReLeaf is American Forests' education and action program that helps individuals, organizations, agencies, and corporations improve the local and global environment by planting and caring for trees.

For information on our distribution, please visit our website
www.oroeditions.com

Skyon
Gurgaon, India
SORG ARCHITECTS

"The dynamic movement of the tower, both in plan and elevation, gives it a very interesting sculptural form."

–Suman Sorg

PROJECT DESCRIPTION

In the early 1980s the automotive company Maruti Suzuki catapulted Gurgaon from farming village to growing commercial sector, by locating large scale operations there. Lured by tax reforms and the proximity of Delhi International Airport, private firms and multi-national corporations began flocking to Gurgaon as the Indian markets opened up to global investment. One decade later, the largely undeveloped land in Gurgaon appealed to developers as the need for a satellite city in Delhi's expanding metropolitan area became increasingly apparent. Gurgaon has been nicknamed the 'Millennium City' and has seen an unparalleled period of development that has significantly outpaced progress on infrastructure and municipal support structures. How to find inspiration from a place still struggling to define its own urban context was a key challenge for Suman Sorg, tasked with the design of the large-scale, multifamily residential project, Skyon. For this commission, Suman found influence in rich cultural and urban landscape of Northern India – from brightly colored textiles to bustling markets to historical landmarks in cities like Jaipur.

Part of a larger township development, Skyon is located at the southeastern edge of Gurgaon in Sector 60 and connects to a 60-meter wide highway by means of a smaller road to the north of the property. When approached by developer IREO to design a housing development on this parcel, Suman understood that controlled density could provide the opportunity for communities to flourish, breathing

life into the commercial and urban explosion of the past two decades. The goal was to design a project that imparted human scale and organization to a cacophonous environment. Suman's objective in the initial planning stages of the project was to provide the client with analysis and options for organizing a diverse set of housing typologies and programmatic amenities. The schemes that emerged included the superblock, in which mid-rises and towers are integrated into larger building clusters; the sculpture park, in which scattered towers are encircled by a base of townhouses; and the common green, in which a single tower anchors one end of a public quadrangle bounded by mid-rise buildings.

The focal point of the common green, the scheme ultimately selected for the site, is a 40-story iconic tower with a pinwheel layout, composed of four stacked units radiating from a rectangular core. This plan for the tower is derived from the Hindu symbol for good luck. Its simple geometric design not only proves advantageous during construction, but affords each unit unobstructed views in three directions. The building's ornamental façade remains a tenant of the architecture, as exterior balconies are modulated to create undulating forms akin to paper origami.

Within each unit, bedrooms and living spaces are pushed toward the outer, fully glazed walls. This contrasts with the opposite wall, which is solid and utilizes a pattern of punched windows to light

the space. Residential balconies extend along the length of the glazed facade, providing extremely effective shading under both high- and low-angle sunlight, thereby reducing the tower's total energy consumption. At night, a subtle wash of light can be seen lighting the inside edge of the tower's four concrete walls by means of hidden LED lights.

Centrally located, Skyon's common green acts as a park for pedestrian circulation and activities. Residential mid-rise buildings ranging from nine to thirteen stories tall border three sides of this central green space. Views from these units are directed either inward to the garden oasis or outward to the nearby mountains. Midrise façades incorporate a generous use of balconies, which rhythmically shift from floor to floor, echoing the tower form. These façades create a dynamic visual foundation upon which the contrasting forms of the slender tower and garden pavilion Clubhouse are further enhanced.

The social center of this development, the Clubhouse includes squash courts, swimming pools, fitness rooms, lounges and a restaurant opening into an adjacent garden. In contrast to the tower design, this building was conceived as a low-lying pavilion, partially sunken and belonging more to the landscape than to its neighboring buildings. The double-curved roof and canted glass exterior remain true to this concept, as do the partially sunken squash courts and atrium stair leading to parking below ground. Throughout the project, cultural influences like Vastu, an ancient concept similar to feng shui that affects interior layouts of spaces, or Rasta, a Hindu reference to holy paths, some of which weave through Gurgaon, can be seen in the design and planning of Skyon's residential buildings. However, more pivotal to the project is its emphasis on community, sustainability and a reclaiming of the pedestrian lifestyle for Gurgaon's ever-growing number of residents.

Delhi and Gurgaon are linked by an eight-lane expressway. At Gurgaon the expressway merges with NH8, the national highway connecting the capital, Delhi, to India's financial hub, Mumbai. In 2010, the New Delhi metro was extended to Gurgaon, providing a much-needed connection to the city. Future expansion for the metro connects Skyon and other developments in the IREO-developed integrated township.

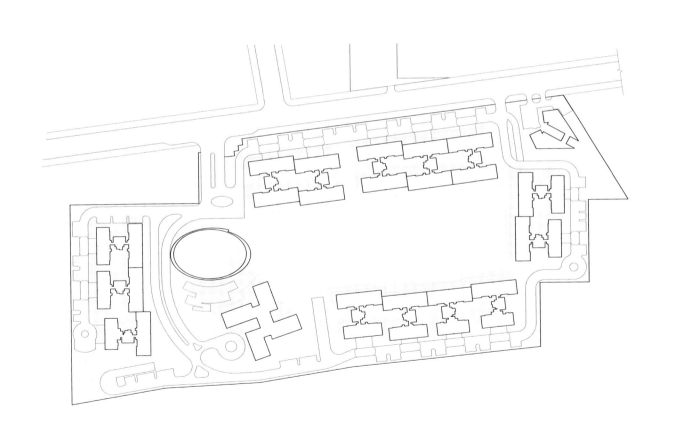

   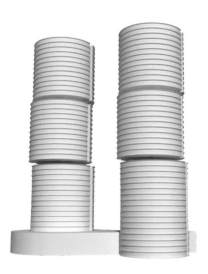

The initial tower design for Sector 60 is rooted in the minaret. Suman draws from the Qutab mausoleum in New Delhi, home to the tallest brick minaret in the world. The minaret's conical shape and ostentatious vertical flutes, visually broken by a series of horizontal bands, offer the illusion that the minaret is taller than it really is. Similar features are employed on early iterations of this residential tower, where balconies form the flutes of the tower and are rotated from floor to floor to create a visual twisting effect.

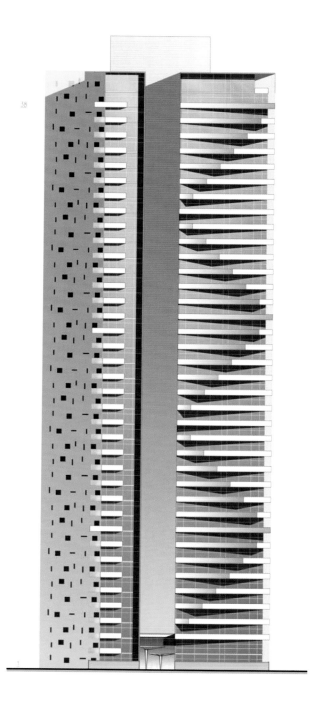

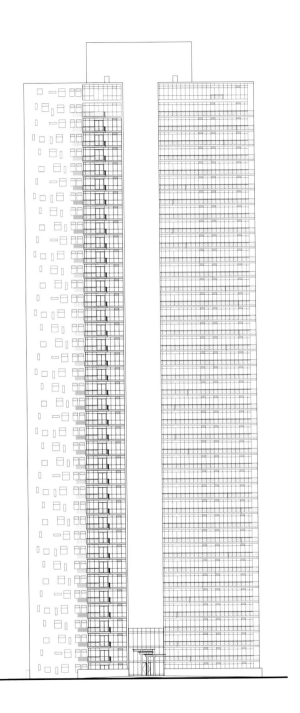

This 40-story tower must not only meet certain sustainable goals, but must be reconciled with the cultural nuances of building in the region. Local fire code dictates that stairs, kitchens, bathrooms and spaces that would typically be pushed toward the interior core, be naturally ventilated. Similarly, designers are required to include service balconies attached to each unit.

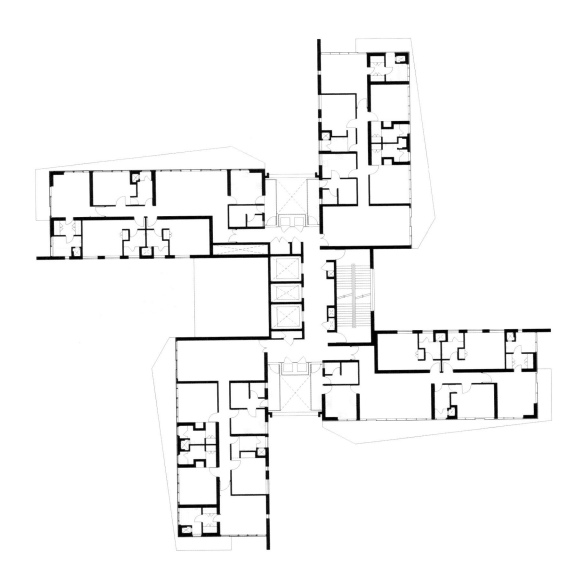

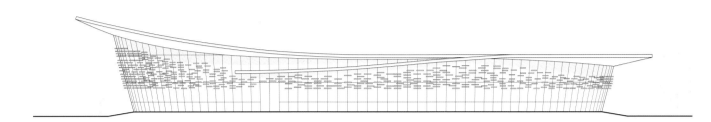

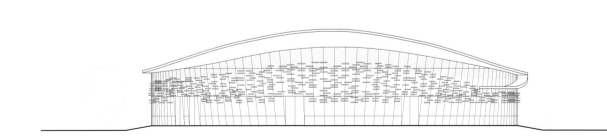

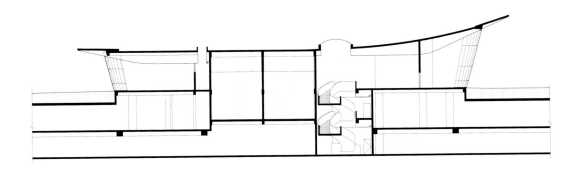

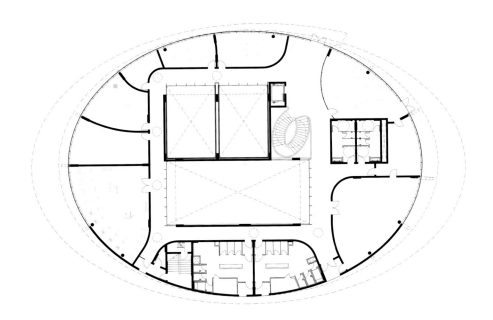

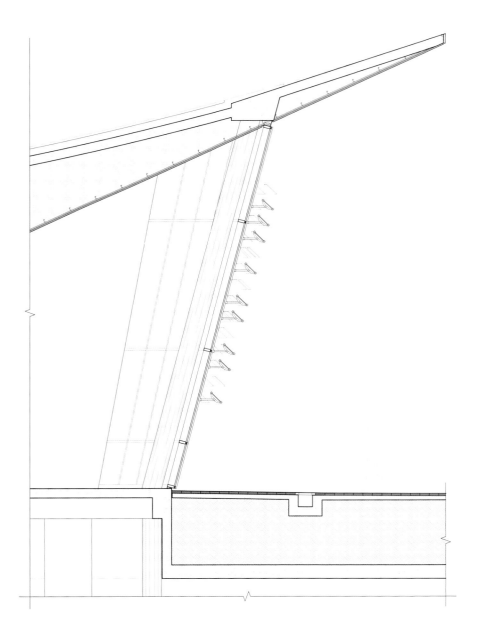

The Clubhouse is designed with several sustainable features in mind. Arrays of photovoltaic (PV) panels are mounted to the mullions of the exterior curtainwall. The patterned arrangement of solar panels mimics the placement of window openings on the nearby tower and provides passive shading in addition to the energy generated by the panels themselves.

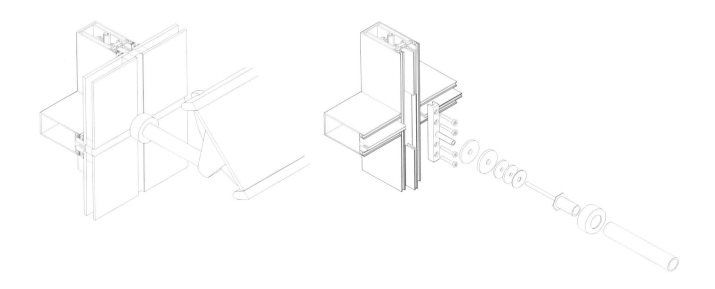

SUMAN SORG, FAIA
Principal

Suman Sorg established her practice in 1986 and it has since become one of the largest solely woman-owned architecture firms in the United States. Under Suman's leadership the firm has amassed an extensive international portfolio of residential, commercial, educational, institutional and civic projects.
Suman's overall philosophy of design is characterized by a strong commitment to thoughtful modern architecture that explores spatial, material and visual experience. Rather than imposing a style irrespective of context, she carefully examines the unique characteristics of each place (site, climate, culture, community), along with programmatic requirements, and looks to this intersection as the catalyst for an architectural concept. A long-standing practice in historic preservation and interest in vernacular architecture compliments her modernist leanings. By combining contemporary techniques and design strategies with the innovative handling of traditional architectural language and indigenous buildings materials, she endeavors to create meaningful architectural compositions that relate to their extended contexts and elevate the spatial, material and visual experience.

Suman emphasizes a philosophy of "light touch," striving for simplicity and clarity of design. She advocates an integrated approach to preserving and protecting the environment which is focused on an examination of project specific relationships to five Sustainability Concepts: context and locality, stakeholders and community, lifecycle solutions, conservation of resources, and designs that work. She believes that when a building serves its function and the people who inhabit it, the project is successful in providing a transparent solution that reflects its human purpose.

Suman Sorg's work has been recognized with numerous honors, including multiple awards from the American Institute of Architects. She has lectured extensively for the AIA, the National Building Museum, the Urban Land Institute, the Center for Architecture in New York, the US Department of State, and the National Trust for Historic Preservation. She is frequently called upon to serve on design panels and juries.
Suman Sorg is a Fellow of the American Institute of Architects and sits on the board of the Washington, DC Building Industry Association. She is a Peer Reviewer for the General Services Administration Design Excellence Program, serves as a trustee for the Beverly Willis Architecture Foundation, and is a member of the Lambda Alpha International Honor Society.
Suman began her studies at the School of Planning and Architecture in New Delhi, India and completed her Bachelor of Architecture at Howard University in Washington, DC. She went on to study Design and Historic Preservation at Cornell University in Ithaca, New York.

Suman lives in Washington, DC and has one daughter, Nikki Sorg, who works with her in her practice.

PROJECT CREDITS

SKYON
GURGAON, INDIA

Client	IREO Management Pvt. Ltd.
Architect	Sorg Architects
Design Architect	Suman Sorg, FAIA
Landscape Architect	M. Paul Friedberg and Partners
Interior Designer	Sorg Architects